THE GENIUS KID'S GUIDE TO

MYTHICAL CREATURES

BY SARA NOVAK

North Star
KIDS

First Edition
First Printing, 2023

 THIS BOOK CONTAINS
RECYCLED MATERIALS

Editor: Brienna Rossiter
Interior Designer: Karli Kruse
Cover Designer: Karli Kruse

ISBN: 978-1-952455-12-4 (paperback)

Library of Congress Control Number: 2022946057

Distributed in paperback by North Star Editions, Inc.
2297 Waters Drive
Mendota Heights, MN 55120
www.northstareditions.com

Printed in the United States of America

Table of Contents

BIGFOOT

A Surprise Sighting

It's a cold fall day. Three friends are hiking through the woods. Their steps crunch the fallen leaves. Thick trees grow on either side of a narrow path. The friends walk single file. Suddenly, the first friend stops and yells. He points to a blurry shape.

Most Bigfoot sightings occur in forests.

Many photos and videos of Bigfoot are blurry.

A huge figure stands on the path ahead of them. Its body is covered in dark, shaggy fur. It's Bigfoot!

For a moment, Bigfoot stares back at the three people. Then the creature turns and runs. It disappears into the trees. One friend tries to take a picture with her camera. But the image just shows a dark blur. Bigfoot has vanished without a trace.

Legends Around the World

Many parts of the world have legends of a huge, hairy beast. In North America, Indigenous people told stories of a wild man. The legend continued as settlers came from Europe. In 1811, a man in Canada found large footprints in the snow. Later, other Canadians said they saw the creature. The monster became known as Sasquatch.

The names Sasquatch and Bigfoot are both used to describe the same creature.

A sign warns hikers of possible Bigfoot sightings.

In the United States, the creature was named Bigfoot. Many sightings occurred in the Pacific Northwest. People claimed to see a creature walking in forests. They said the creature was tall, hairy, and brown. They also said it had very large feet.

FUN FACT
Ape-like beasts appear in stories from around the world. Australia is said to be the home of the Yowie. In parts of Asia, legends tell of the Almas.

A similar creature exists in Asian folklore. This creature is called the yeti. Like Bigfoot, it has a hairy body and giant feet. But a yeti's fur can be white, gray, or reddish brown.

According to legend, yetis live in the Himalayas. These mountains run through several countries in South Asia. The mountains are very tall and cold. The yeti's thick fur keeps it warm.

FUN FACT
In Tibet, a yeti is called a *metoh-kangmi*. This name means "man-bear snow-man."

The yeti is a large monster that can weigh hundreds of pounds.

Story Spotlight

The yeti comes from folktales told by the Sherpa people. These people are native to Nepal, Tibet, and India. They live high in the mountains. By the 1900s, mountain climbing had become a popular sport. Many people came to climb the Himalayas. Climbers often hired Sherpa people to be their guides. The climbers heard stories of yetis. Many climbers believed the creatures were real. They spread the stories around the world.

The Himalayas run through India, Tibet, and Nepal. Mount Everest, the highest peak in the world, is part of these mountains.

Bigfoot Traits

Bigfoot has thick hair all over his body. He is very tall. And he weighs hundreds of pounds. Although he looks like an ape, Bigfoot walks on two legs like a human. Some people who see Bigfoot say he acts like a human, too. Others say he acts like an ape. For example, Bigfoot does not use words to speak. Instead, he makes a loud, animal-like scream. In many stories, Bigfoot stays away from people.

In some stories, yetis are shy, too. People often find only their footprints. Other stories tell of yetis interacting with people.

FUN FACT
Some people think Bigfoot eats meat. Others say he only eats plants.

Some stories say Bigfoot is 9 feet (2.7 m) tall.

Some versions of yetis are extremely scary. Others are less dangerous.

In many of these stories, yetis are dangerous. They attack people and animals. Yetis are very strong. They can hurt people and kill livestock. However, yetis aren't always mean. In some legends, they protect the mountains. The legends say yetis are spirits. They live in mountain forests. The yetis can influence how well people hunt.

FUN FACT
Some legends say the yeti's feet point backward. This helps it walk up mountains.

Searching for Proof

Many people have tried to find Bigfoot. Some say they have seen the ape-like creature. They may even claim to have photos or videos.

The most famous footage of Bigfoot is known as the Patterson film. The 1967 film shows a creature walking through a forest. The creature's gait is different than a human's. It lifts its legs higher. The figure is also hunched over. The film matches other Bigfoot sightings. But many people believe the film is fake.

Other people claim they have found Bigfoot's footprints. Most Bigfoot prints are 16 to 18 inches (41 to 46 cm) long. Some are as wide as 7 inches (18 cm). Some prints show small lines and ridges. These details are different from a human's foot. Other prints have

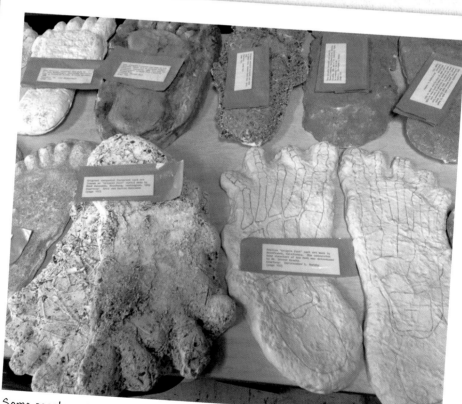

Some people make casts of footprints supposedly made by Bigfoot. They press material into a print to show its shape.

Sightings that people think are Bigfoot sometimes turn out to be bears.

only three or four toes. Some people think a print with these details could not be a hoax. But most scientists don't believe Bigfoot really made the prints.

Some people claim to find bits of Bigfoot's hair or skin. Scientists have studied these samples. The scientists proved that the hairs came from humans or other animals. Similarly, many people claim to find yeti footprints or body parts.

However, scientists don't think yetis exist. Scientists tested the body parts. All were from bears or other animals. The footprints could have been from bears as well. When bears walk, their back paws sometimes step on part of their front-paw prints. The combined prints look similar to an ape's.

FUN FACT

In 1951, a mountain climber took a photo of a footprint on Mount Everest. The huge print was about 13 inches (33 cm) long. Some people think a yeti made it.

CENTAUR

On the Hunt

Centaurs stand on a tall hill. Some carry giant rocks. Others have clubs made of big branches. Several boars graze in a field down below.

The centaurs sprint down the hill. They scream and cheer as they run. Their hooves kick up dirt and grass. Each step thumps like a drum.

The boars try to run. But it's too late. The centaurs catch them all. The hunt is a success! The centaurs will eat well tonight.

Art and stories about centaurs often involve hunting.

In some stories, centaurs fight with clubs. Others shoot arrows from bows.

Centaur Traits

A centaur is half human and half horse. The creature is human from the waist up. It has the body and legs of a horse.

Centaurs come from Greek mythology. In early stories, centaurs tend to be wild. They are strong but not very smart. But stories about centaurs have changed over time. In later stories, centaurs are more intelligent. Many are good at archery. This is the skill of shooting arrows with a bow.

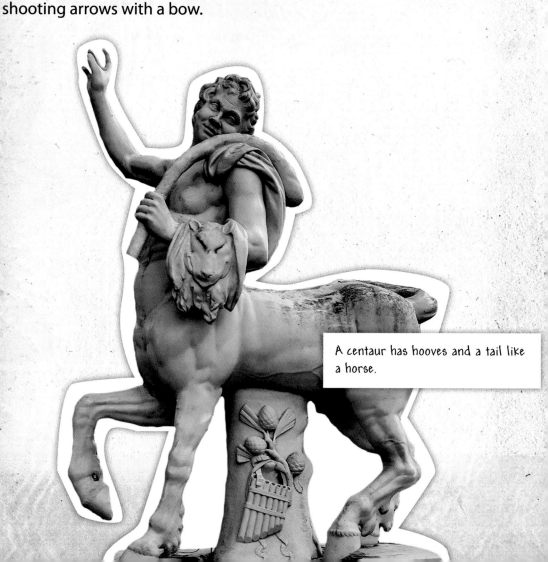

A centaur has hooves and a tail like a horse.

Story Spotlight

Greek myths say the first centaur was the son of an evil king. The king betrayed Zeus, the ruler of the gods. Zeus punished the king. He sent the king to the underworld. But the centaur survived. His children grew up to be rude and violent.

In modern stories, centaurs are often skilled warriors.

Centaur Behavior

According to legends, centaurs live in Thessaly. This region is in northern Greece. Centaurs roam its mountains, caves, and forests.

In Greek myths, centaurs often behave badly. They start wild fights. Some even try to kidnap people. But not all centaurs are violent. Chiron is an example. He was very wise. He helped and taught many great heroes. He also had the power to heal.

The Greek hero Hercules fought a wicked centaur.

The centaur Chiron taught the hero Achilles how to use a bow.

FUN FACT
Centaurus is a constellation in the night sky. One legend says it honors Chiron. The gods placed him in the stars after he died.

An Explanation?

The people of Thessaly may have inspired legends of centaurs. The Thessalians raised horses. They were skilled riders.

In one sport, a man chased a bull while riding a horse. When he got close to the bull, he jumped onto its back. He grabbed its horns. Then he wrestled it to the ground.

People may have seen Thessalians riding. These people may not have seen horses before. They may have thought the riders were monsters.

Riding horses became an important part of life in ancient Greece and the surrounding areas.

Story Spotlight

The Thessalians didn't invent horseback riding. People in Central Asia had tamed horses by 3500 BCE. The Greeks started riding horses more than 1,000 years after that. Greek soldiers began using horses around 1500 BCE. The horses pulled chariots. Riding came later. Greek soldiers began riding horses into battle in 900 BCE.

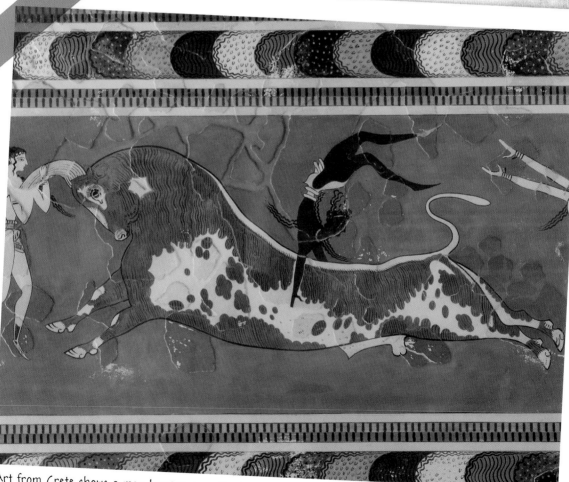

Art from Crete shows a man leaping over the back of a bull.

CHUPACABRA

Out for Blood

A farmer sits on her porch. Suddenly, she hears her chickens clucking loudly. She runs to her chicken coop. The farmer sees a terrifying beast. It has sharp fangs and patchy fur. It's a chupacabra!

The chupacabra is a monster that supposedly attacks and kills animals.

Most chupacabra attacks happen in places without many people.

The beast grabs a chicken with its claws. It turns to stare at the farmer. Its eyes glow. Then it runs off into the woods. For now, the rest of the chickens are safe.

FUN FACT
The chupacabra dislikes bright lights. It usually attacks at night.

Spreading the Legend

The chupacabra is a monster. It attacks livestock such as goats, pigs, and cows. People say it drains animals' blood. It bites their necks and leaves small holes.

Chupacabra legends began in the 1990s. The earliest stories came from Puerto Rico. People reported attacks on livestock. They believed a monster was to blame.

Since then, many people have said they've seen the creature. The sightings come from all over North and South America. They often happen near farms and forests.

FUN FACT
Chupacabra means "goat-sucker" in Spanish.

Like a vampire, the chupacabra uses fangs to suck blood.

Story Spotlight

The chupacabra is a cryptid. A cryptid is an animal that people claim to see but can't prove is real. The chupacabra is one of many creatures people claim to see. The Loch Ness Monster is another. Loch Ness is a lake in Scotland. Legend says a monster lurks in its waters. Scientists think the Loch Ness Monster is just made-up. But some people travel to the lake. They try to see the monster.

People posted about chupacabras online. Stories of the strange beast spread far and wide. The rumors changed as they spread. They also helped the creature gain attention.

People have claimed to see chupacabras in barns and other places where animals live.

Chupacabra Traits

In most stories, chupacabras are less than 5 feet (1.5 m) tall. They have red eyes. They also have long claws and fangs. Some people say chupacabras have spikes along their backs.

Some people say the chupacabra has green skin like a frog's.

People in Texas have claimed to see a dog-like creature killing animals.

Early stories said the chupacabra looked like a furry lizard. The creature stood on its back legs. Later, the stories changed. People began saying the monster walked on all fours. They said it looked more like a dog.

Some people say chupacabras are aliens. There have been UFO sightings near some of the attacks. Other people think the monsters are a science experiment gone wrong.

FUN FACT
Chupacabras are said to smell like rotten eggs.

An Explanation?

In the 2000s, some people claimed to find dead chupacabras. Scientists decided to test the bodies. They found that most of them were actually coyotes. The tests also found that the coyotes had been sick. They had a disease called mange.

Mange makes an animal's skin itch. The animal scratches itself. Its fur starts to fall out. Soon, it looks ragged and patchy. People may have seen some of these strange-looking animals and thought they were monsters.

FUN FACT

Mites that cause mange can also affect humans. They give humans a rash called scabies.

Coyotes live in the places where people have said they've seen chupacabras.

Story Spotlight

Mange is caused by tiny mites. These mites live on hair and skin. Animals with bad cases of mange can become bony and hairless. They can also become weak. Normally, coyotes hunt rabbits and deer. However, livestock would be easier for them to catch. For this reason, weak coyotes might attack livestock instead.

In the dark, an animal that is sick with mange might look like a monster.

The mites that cause mange are microscopic.

DRAGON

Beware the Dragon

High in the mountains, all is quiet. A dragon naps on a nest of sticks and weeds. Three golden eggs lie beneath her enormous green body. The dragon keeps the eggs warm. She dreams of dragon hatchlings soon to come.

Dragons may make their homes in mountains or other places far from people.

In fantasy stories, dragons and knights are often enemies.

A rustle of leaves wakes the dragon. Her head snaps up. She sees a flash of silver. A knight has come to fight her. He wants to protect his village from the fiery beast. Many brave knights have tried before and failed.

The knight raises his sword high. The dragon opens her mouth and breathes a blast of fire. The battle begins.

History of Dragons

Dragons are mighty mythical creatures. People have told stories about dragons for thousands of years. No one knows how dragon stories came to be. Some scientists think ancient people found dinosaur bones. Back then, people did not know about dinosaurs. They may have thought the bones belonged to dragons.

Scientists found one of the oldest dragon images in a Chinese tomb. The image may be 6,000 years old. The piece of art was made from colored seashells.

In Western stories, dragons may attack castles or villages.

In China, red dragons stand for happiness, passion, and creativity.

Other dragon images appear on old maps. Hundreds of years ago, some people thought the world was flat. They believed dragons lived at the edge of the world.

Stories about dragons vary, depending on what part of the world they come from. In Western countries, dragons are fierce fire-breathers. The West includes countries in Europe, North America, and South America. In Eastern countries, dragons are wise and powerful serpents. The East includes countries in Asia.

FUN FACT
In a Greek myth, a prince planted dragon teeth in the ground. The teeth grew into an army of fierce warriors.

Dragon Appearance

Dragons in Western countries are frightening creatures. They have huge, lizard-like bodies. These dragons have long necks, sharp claws, and strong tails. Scales cover the beasts from head to tail. The dragons' scales are often a mix of colors. They can be red, blue, green, silver, or gold.

Western dragons have two wings. Most Western dragons have four legs. But others have only two legs. Some dragons with two legs are called wyverns. Wyverns also have spiked tails.

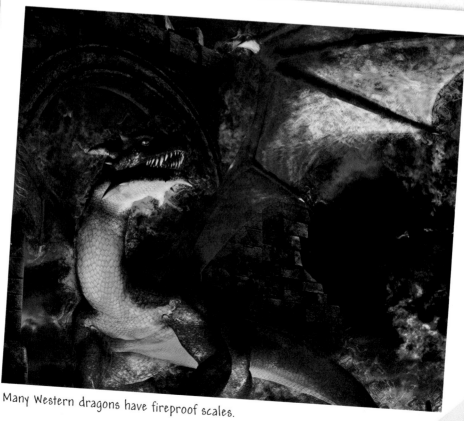

Many Western dragons have fireproof scales.

Dragons can use their sharp teeth and claws to attack.

Many Eastern dragons chase after a red ball, or pearl. The pearl gives them wisdom.

Dragons in Eastern countries have long bodies and very short legs. Most Eastern dragons don't have wings. However, some of them can fly.

People compare Eastern dragons to many animals. The dragon's head looks like the head of a camel. Its body looks like a snake. The dragon also has claws like an eagle and scales like a fish.

Eastern dragons can be almost any color. Images often show the dragons with wide-open mouths. This makes it seem as if the dragons are laughing.

FUN FACT

In China, people make dragon puppets from wood and cloth. They perform dragon dances in parades to celebrate the Lunar New Year.

Story Spotlight

Dragons appear in many Chinese myths and legends. In these stories, dragons have many magical powers. They can make themselves as small as a worm. Or they can grow as large as the world. Some Chinese dragons turn into water or fire. Others can become invisible or glow in the dark.

In a dragon dance, people use poles to handle a long, colorful dragon puppet.

Dragon Behavior

Many dragons make their homes in caves, mountains, or forests. But some prefer to live by rivers or lakes. Dragons usually live with other dragons. Communities of dragons are known as weyrs. Weyrs grow when female dragons lay eggs. Female dragons sit on their nests to protect the eggs.

Western dragons are wicked and dangerous. They breathe fire and have poisonous breath. Hungry dragons might eat sheep, cows, or humans. They guard piles of treasure, such as gold or jewels. Some stories mention castles, knights, and princesses. Dragons in these stories fight humans to protect themselves.

Many dragons fly high above the ground. Large wings help them cover long distances.

Some dragons collect and hide treasure in caves and dungeons.

Eastern dragons are water spirits. These dragons rule over oceans and lakes. They breathe clouds and mist. They also control the weather. In many stories, Eastern dragons help and protect humans. They bring humans good luck.

FUN FACT
Southeast Asian folklore tells of dragon-like creatures called nagas. Nagas have snake-like bodies and human heads.

DWARF

At the Forge

A forge burns deep inside a mountain. Coals shine bright in the hot fire. A stocky dwarf blows air onto them. The flames roar. The coals grow hotter. Soon they are ready for the dwarf to use.

The dwarf sticks a long pole into the flames. The pole has a lump of metal at one end. This end turns bright red.

The dwarf removes the hot metal from the fire. He walks carefully to his anvil. Then he hits the metal with a hammer. Slowly, he shapes the metal into a weapon. He forms a short handle and a large hammerhead. It will be a powerful weapon.

A forge is a very hot fire used for melting and shaping metal.

Hot metal shoots out sparks when it is hit with a hammer.

History of Dwarfs

Many stories of dwarfs come from Scandinavia. Some of these stories are thousands of years old. Many are part of the Edda. The Edda is a collection of stories. They come from Norse mythology. These stories were told out loud for many years. In 1223, people began writing them down.

In many of the stories, dwarfs interact with the gods. Sometimes, they fight. Other times, dwarfs have things the gods need. For example, dwarfs often built weapons for the gods. One dwarf made

Illustrations in the Edda show many kinds of creatures.

Dwarfs gave the god Thor a hammer called Mjollnir.

a magic ship. The ship could sail on water or air. When not in use, the ship could fold up. It fit in a pocket.

Dwarfs are also part of the Norse creation story. In this story, the world was made from the body of a giant. Maggots grew in his skull. They wriggled around in the dirt. The gods changed the maggots into dwarfs. The dwarfs looked similar to humans. But they lived underground or in rocks.

Other cultures have their own stories of dwarfs. Some of these dwarfs live underground. Others live in forests.

43

Dwarf Traits

Dwarfs are best known for their short height. They are usually the size of a human child. Some dwarfs have hunched backs that make them even shorter.

Dwarfs' bodies are broad and strong. They often have long beards. In many stories, they look like old men. They often wear hats.

In Norse mythology, dwarfs live in their own realm. It is a world of darkness. It is almost all underground. Systems of tunnels join

Dwarfs often look similar to gnomes.

Sometimes dwarfs find trolls or other monsters in their tunnels.

everything together. Dwarfs dig mines. There, they search for metals and jewels.

In other stories, dwarfs live in the same world as humans. But they still live mostly underground. These dwarfs often make their homes in mountains. They dig tunnels through the rock.

FUN FACT
The northern lights are waves of colors that flash across the night sky. One legend says dwarfs cause them with their cooking fires.

Story Spotlight

J. R. R. Tolkien wrote several famous fantasy novels. His books feature many magical creatures, including dwarfs. The dwarfs in Tolkien's books live deep underground. They have entire cities and kingdoms underneath mountains. Tolkien's dwarfs are stocky and strong. They can live a long time. Many of them are warriors. They fight in huge battles. They may use swords, shields, axes, or hammers.

Dwarfs create strong chain mail and beautiful jewelry.

In some stories, dwarfs wear helmets and armor.

Dwarfs use forges to do metalwork. First, they heat the metal in a fire. Then, they pound the hot metal with a hammer. They shape it into tools or weapons. For example, they often make swords and rings. Many of these objects have magical powers. Dwarfs sometimes give these objects as gifts to gods.

In one story, dwarfs made a gold boar. It was covered in tiny gold hairs. And it was very shiny. The boar shone so bright that it could turn night into day.

FUN FACT
In some stories, dwarfs can be invisible. In others, they can shape-shift.

Dwarf Behavior

Dwarfs tend to live in groups. They build huge halls and cities. The walls and buildings are made of stone. Many dwarfs love their homes. They will fight bravely to defend them.

Dwarfs like shiny things. They fill their halls with gold. They also decorate their homes with jewels.

Dwarfs spend a lot of time at their forges. They can make many beautiful objects. But they have other skills, too. Some stories say dwarfs are wise. They know many secrets. Sometimes, dwarfs can even see the future.

Gods and humans visit dwarfs to ask for help. The dwarfs often provide useful gifts or advice. But they may punish people who try to steal from them. Other dwarfs try to avoid humans.

In some legends, dwarfs are evil. They steal food. They even kidnap women and children. They drag these people back to their tunnels. In some cases, the humans never return home.

However, most stories say dwarfs are kind and helpful. For example, some dwarfs help farmers. If animals get lost, dwarfs herd them back to the farm. Dwarfs may also share food with people. They make people's lives easier.

FUN FACT

Miners sometimes left gifts of food for dwarfs. They hoped these gifts would keep the dwarfs from getting angry.

Dwarfs' underground kingdoms can have towering buildings.

FAIRY

A Visit to Fairyland

Deep in the woods, a girl discovers a secret land. The area is lush and green. Music fills the flower-scented air. Fairies called Little Folk fly above and around her.

In some stories, humans can get lost in fairyland forever.

Many fairies enjoy playing instruments such as the flute.

The fairies welcome the girl. They give her gifts of fairy food. With each delicious bite, she feels sleepier and sleepier. She is falling under the fairies' spell.

When the girl awakes, the Little Folk are dancing around her. The fairy dance seems to last only a few minutes. But with each step of the dance, years pass. The girl can't escape. Life as she knew it will never be the same.

FUN FACT
Many stories say that fairies love music. The fairies often hold hands and dance in a circle.

History of Fairies

Stories of fairies appear in folklore around the world. In many stories, fairies are known as the Little Folk. They live in a secret world. Sometimes, humans stumble upon fairyland by accident.

People have told fairy stories for thousands of years. In the Middle Ages, fairy stories became very popular. Stories often came from Scotland, England, and Ireland.

Most fairy myths take place in nature. Long ago, humans told stories about spirits to explain nature. For example, some people thought fairy dances caused flowers to grow faster. Others believed that fairies controlled the weather.

FUN FACT
In Irish folklore, a fairy carried stones in her apron. As she dropped the stones, mountains formed.

Fairies may look like glowing spots of light in the air.

Story Spotlight

In stories from Scotland, a fairy named Gentle Annie creates storms. These storms cause trouble for people fishing at sea. Another Scottish story tells of a blue-faced winter fairy. This fairy covers the land with snow. A third tale said dancing fairies formed the northern lights. These fairies were called Merry Dancers.

In other stories, fairies guard animals. They protect deer and wolves in the wild. Fairies might also guard water. They keep streams from overflowing.

Water fairies protect the animals in the water, such as frogs and fish.

Types of Fairies

Fairies take many forms. In stories today, fairies tend to be small. They often have wings. But in old folklore, fairies were taller than humans. They were wingless. Many fairies were also invisible.

Oftentimes, fairies blend in with their surroundings. Woodland fairies tend to be brown and green. They blend in with leaves and trees. Water fairies are blue and green. They blend in with ponds.

Some fairies have scales and plants growing on their skin.

Forest fairies like to sit on the tops of mushrooms.

Fairies are also shape-shifters. They often take the forms of animals. Some fairies appear as wolves or horses. Others look like birds. One type of fairy looks like a young girl. But she has scales and fish-like hands.

According to folklore, there are many types of fairies. Undines look like humans. But they have shiny, blue-green skin. Sylph fairies are invisible. They glow as they fly. Other fairies are not so beautiful. Barghests have horns, claws, and big teeth.

The brownie is a Scottish fairy that lives in humans' houses. This type of fairy stands 3 feet (0.9 m) tall. Brownies have shaggy hair. They often dress in raggedy brown clothes.

A fairy's appearance often helps it hide from humans. Since fairies can take many forms, they are hard for people to spot. In stories, humans often do not recognize fairies.

FUN FACT
The Gooseberry Wife is a fairy that appears as a giant, hairy caterpillar. She guards gooseberry patches.

Leprechauns are a type of fairy from Ireland.

A brownie washes dishes in a human's home.

Fairies often live together in large,
hollowed-out trees.

Fairy Behavior

Fairies live in secret. They only reveal themselves to humans when they want to. However, many fairies like the company of other fairies. Trooping fairies live in groups. Solitary fairies live alone.

Fairies are skilled in many trades. Common fairy jobs include spinning, weaving, and cooking. Fairies often sing while they work. And they always clean up. They like things to be neat and orderly.

Fairies depend on humans for many things. For example, fairies may take grain to make cakes. They also borrow tools for their trades. They might take spinning wheels and weaving looms.

Some fairies are kind and generous. But others like to cause trouble. To trick humans, fairies use a magical power called glamour. Glamour makes humans see things that are not real. Breaking the spell can be hard. It requires an ointment made of four-leaf clovers. Humans rub the ointment on their eyes.

In fairy stories, humans must be careful. They don't know if they can trust fairies. People might fall under fairy spells. Or they might get stuck in fairyland. In some stories, however, humans and fairies are friends.

FUN FACT
Knockers are fairies that work in mines. They knock on the walls to lead humans toward silver and gold.

GENIE

A Magic Lamp

A young boy stumbles across the desert. A strong wind whips up clouds of sand. Squinting his eyes, the boy spots a cave. He runs inside to escape the storm.

The boy walks through a narrow tunnel. Suddenly, the tunnel widens. A large room lies up ahead. Treasure covers its floor. The boy

In some stories, genies appear when people rub the sides of lamps.

Genies often appear in a puff of smoke.

takes a step toward the treasure. But he trips over a lamp on the ground.

The boy picks up the lamp. He wipes its side with his sleeve. Smoke pours from the lamp, and a huge genie appears. The genie thanks the boy for freeing him. He gives the boy a wish as a reward.

FUN FACT
In addition to lamps, genies can be trapped in jewelry, pots, or jars.

History of Genies

Genies are based on tales of creatures called jinn. Jinn come from Arab mythology. They are invisible. And they can do magic.

Stories of jinn are very old. People told them out loud for many years. The stories changed and spread over time. Later, some of them were written down.

Many books tell stories of jinn. *One Thousand and One Nights* is a famous example. This book is a collection of stories. The stories came from Asia, North Africa, and the Middle East. People gathered the stories together. They also made new versions.

Stories of jinn date back to at least 2400 BCE.

One main story links all the tales in *One Thousand and One Nights*. A woman tells the tales to a king.

Story Spotlight

Today, many genies have blue skin. The movie
Aladdin helped make this coloring popular.
Disney made this movie in the 1990s. The
movie used colors as symbols. Blues and greens
were for good characters. Bad characters were
red or orange. The genie helped Aladdin. So,
artists made him blue. Later in the movie, a bad
character turns into a genie. That genie is red.

People changed stories about genies to reflect their own cultures and ideas.

In the 1700s, Antoine Galland translated the stories into French. He used the word *génie* to refer to jinn. He also added some stories. One was "Aladdin and the Magic Lamp." In this story, a boy finds a lamp. A genie is inside. The genie helps Aladdin. He grants wishes for the boy.

Many people read Galland's book. It became very popular. And it shaped how stories about genies spread. In the original stories, most jinn were free and powerful. But stories in Europe began to change. They were more like Galland's stories. For example, they used the word *genie*. They also had genies serve people and grant wishes. However, the genies could still be tricky.

In some stories, genies are trapped in bottles. They try to trick people into letting them out.

FUN FACT
In early versions, the story of Aladdin took place in China. Later versions changed the setting.

Genie Traits

Both jinn and genies are invisible most of the time. But people do sometimes see them. Jinn often show up to trick people. They have the power to shape-shift. They can take the form of many animals. Snakes are common choices. So are lions and wolves. Jinn can also choose to look like humans.

Most genies appear when people find or call them. Many genies are trapped in objects, such as lamps, bottles, or rings. The object's owner controls the genie.

Genies and jinn can take many different forms.

Some legends say jinn live in caves in the desert.

An owner can make the genie do magic. But the owner must guard the object carefully. If someone else takes it, the genie will belong to that person instead.

In contrast, jinn are usually wild and free. Some jinn stay away from people. They live in lonely places, such as deserts or ruins. Others live in or near people's homes. In some cases, jinn get trapped in objects. These jinn can sometimes be controlled by humans.

One story tells of a king who captured many jinn. He kept them in jars. He made them build and fight for him. He became rich and powerful. Many years later, a man was fishing. He found one of the jars. He opened it. One of the jinn appeared. He tried to kill the man. But the man tricked him. The man got him to go back into the jar.

FUN FACT
In some stories, people cast spells to control jinn.

Magical Powers

In early stories, jinn have great power. They can do magic. Stories also say they can fly or time-travel. In some ways, jinn are like ghosts. They can haunt places. And they can possess people. Sometimes they even appear in people's dreams.

Jinn can use their powers for good or evil. Bad jinn can make people sick. Good jinn heal people. Some jinn guard treasure. They may hurt people who try to take it. Or they can give it away. But first, they often make people pass a test.

Jinn may guard treasure that is hidden in caves or buried underground.

In Western stories, genies are often friendly and helpful.

People can ask jinn for luck or help. But they must be careful. In many stories, jinn are dangerous. They like causing trouble. They hurt or trick people. As a result, stories about them tend to be scary.

Most genies in Western stories have less power. Many genies must serve humans. Some can grant only three wishes. Problems can still come up. Wishes can have consequences people didn't plan on. Or genies can make mistakes. Even so, the stories tend to be less scary. They can even be funny.

Legends of genies continue to change. Sometimes legends blend together. Western ideas about genies are used in movies around the world. And scary jinn appear in a few Western movies and games.

GIANT

In the Land of Giants

A giant wanders slowly through the forest. He is nearly as tall as the trees. The giant lifts his heavy ax. He chops down a tree with just two swings. Its huge trunk crashes to the ground.

Stories say a giant's footprints can make craters or lakes.

Statues of Paul Bunyan and his ox stand in Bemidji, Minnesota.

The giant cuts down several more trees. He ties the trunks together. Then he picks them all up. The giant carries them to a clearing. There, he starts building a cabin. The giant piles up logs to make the walls. Then he adds a roof. By evening, the cabin is finished. The giant smiles and walks inside.

FUN FACT
One legend tells of a giant named Paul Bunyan. He had a pet ox named Babe.

History of Giants

People have been telling stories about giants for thousands of years. Some famous myths come from Greece and Norway. In Norse myths, giants were the parents of the gods. Over time, the giants and gods became enemies. They fought against one another. Each wanted more power. But the gods were stronger. They took over.

People in Greece also told stories of gods fighting giants. The Greek gods fought a long war against the

FUN FACT
Norse myths say there will be more fighting between giants and gods. One day, this huge battle will end the world.

Many myths tell of giants fighting battles.

A painting from a Mongolian temple shows Pan Gu (left) separating the land and sky.

giants. The gods won. The giants were buried under the mountains. They were trapped. But they were not dead. Some people believed these giants caused earthquakes. The giants were also said to make volcanoes shoot out fire.

Many other cultures have stories about giants, too. Some explain how the world was created. For example, Chinese myths tell of a giant named Pan Gu. He was born inside an egg. He split the egg's shell in two. One part became heaven. The other became the earth.

In some versions of this myth, Pan Gu's body turned into the soil. His hair became plants. His eyes became the sun and moon. Other versions say he carved out the land and oceans.

Giant Traits

Giants are known for their great size. In many stories, giants are more than 40 feet (12 m) tall. They tower over humans. And they are very strong. Some giants can pull trees up from the ground. Giants can also throw huge stones.

Some giants can grow to be hundreds of feet tall.

Story Spotlight

People sometimes use legends of giants to explain parts of nature. One example comes from Northern Ireland. A legend tells of a giant named Finn McCool. He wanted to reach a nearby island where another giant lived. Finn built a bridge. He placed thousands of stones in the sea. They made a path toward the island. The group of rocks really exists. It's known as the Giant's Causeway. Scientists think it was formed by lava.

The Giant's Causeway is a bridge-like group of rocks in Northern Ireland. Legends say a giant made it.

Some giants look similar to humans. Other giants are more like monsters. Many giants are fierce fighters. Others are good at building. They can make mountains, islands, and rivers. Some stories tell of giants fishing for whales.

In some myths, giants' bodies are made of ice or stone.

A cyclops is a one-eyed giant that eats people.

Norse myths describe several kinds of giants. There are frost giants, fire giants, and giants that live in the ocean. Some of them have multiple heads. Many have magical powers. For example, some can turn into animals such as wolves.

Many giants live in groups. The biggest giant is in charge. Other giants live alone. Some giants live in castles. They collect animals and treasure. Some try to trap people, too.

In Greek stories, some giants have only one eye. This type of giant is called a cyclops. It often has a herd of sheep. Other Greek myths describe two-eyed giants. These giants fight against the gods.

FUN FACT
The Greek god Zeus throws bolts of lightning. Myths say giants made the bolts.

Giant Behavior

In Norse mythology, some giants were smart and brave. One giant could fight against an entire army of humans. Some giants even tried to duel the gods.

Other giants were not as smart. For example, one Norse myth tells of a giant named Hrungnir. He was huge and strong. He was also mean. His heart was made of stone. So was his head. As a result, he was not very smart.

In general, giants tend not to be very intelligent. People often trick them. In one story, a hero was trapped in a giant's castle. He challenged the giant to an eating contest. The hero hid a bag under

Giants can be fierce and stubborn. They can also be quick to start fights.

In some legends, giants guard mountains or forests.

his shirt. Instead of eating, he stuffed food into it. The trick worked. The giant ate so much he could not move. The hero escaped.

Some giants are dangerous. In North America, a Paiute legend describes giants with red hair. These giants attack people and eat them. Filipino myths also tell of a giant that eats people.

However, not all giants are evil. In Spain, stories say a giant owned two castles. He was kind and took care of people. Another giant carved toys for children. People around the world continue to create new stories about giants.

FUN FACT
A British legend tells of twin giants. Their names were Gog and Magog. These brave giants helped people.

GNOME

Master Gardeners

A full moon shines on the garden. Several gnomes walk through the bushes. Their tools clank. The gnomes come out each night to take care of the plants.

Gnomes use magic to help flowers stay healthy and beautiful.

Gnomes use tools such as watering cans and shovels to care for plants.

The gnomes yank weeds from the dirt. They check each flower. A few flowers have wilted. Their leaves droop.

The gnomes touch the stems. Magic flows through their fingertips. Each plant's leaves become greener. The petals perk up, too.

The gnomes work hard to keep the garden clean. They trim branches. They pick up sticks from the grass.

Soon, dawn approaches. The gnomes duck back into the dirt. They don't want anyone to know that they have been working.

FUN FACT
In some stories, gnomes are statues that come to life at night.

Spreading the Legend

Many people associate gnomes with gardens. But that is not how stories of gnomes first started. The kind of work that gnomes do has changed over time. Early legends said gnomes were miners. They worked underground. People believed gnomes led human miners through tunnels. The gnomes showed the miners where to dig.

Many of these early stories came from the Netherlands and Germany. The stories may have been inspired by tales of other beings. These beings include dwarfs, fairies, and trolls. Gnomes share some traits with them. For example, all tend to be small. And they can often do magic.

In most stories, gnomes are not dangerous. Instead, they often help humans.

Story Spotlight

Garden gnomes became popular decorations in Europe in the 1840s. People still place statues of gnomes in their gardens today. The largest collection of garden gnomes is at the Gnome Reserve. This garden is in England. It has more than 2,000 garden gnomes. Its owners say the gnomes take care of the garden. People come to see the gnomes. They also admire the beautiful flowers and plants.

Gnomes have been linked to gardens for many years.

Over time, people moved to new places. They brought their legends. The stories changed as they spread. Most legends still said gnomes lived underground. But the gnomes were no longer miners. Instead, they took care of the earth. They helped trees and gardens grow.

Meanwhile, other cultures told their own stories of gnome-like creatures. These creatures often lived in forests or under the ground. In some stories, they were builders. Others were said to help people on farms. They cared for plants and animals.

FUN FACT
Hawaiian stories tell of gnomes called 'e'epa. The 'e'epa built a temple in the forest for the gods.

In some stories, gnomes make their homes out of mushrooms.

Some gnomes that live in forests can talk to animals.

Gnome Traits

In many stories, gnomes are short and round. They are often less than 2 feet (0.6 m) tall. Some gnomes are just a few inches tall. Some are a bit taller. But gnomes are never as tall as humans.

Over time, some descriptions of gnomes changed. Many older stories only talked about male gnomes. These gnomes had hunched backs. Their skin was wrinkled. They also had long, white beards.

Later stories describe both male and female gnomes. These gnomes often have big heads and small bodies. Many have large noses, too. One story says gnomes look like potatoes with legs.

Scandinavian gnomes tend to have long, white beards.

Young gnomes appear more often in newer art and stories.

In newer stories, gnomes wear clothes with bright colors. Blue, red, and green are the most common colors. Gnomes tend to wear pointed hats as well.

In some stories, gnomes are quiet and shy. They try to avoid people. For example, one story tells of small men that hide in trees. When a person sees the small men, they stop time and disappear.

Other gnomes are friendly and fun. In Scandinavia, gnomes are associated with Christmas. They are said to bring people presents. These gnomes can make friends with people. But they can also play tricks.

FUN FACT
In Scandinavia, gnomes can have many names. A gnome may be called a tomte, nisse, or tonttu.

Gnome Behavior

Most stories say gnomes live in groups. In one story, gnomes have a king. His name is Gob. He leads the gnomes. They live together in huge palaces made of stone. These palaces are underground.

Groups of gnomes sometimes live together in places called Gnome Eggs. These round structures sit above the ground. A Gnome Egg is invisible to most people. But inside, it looks like a castle. Tunnels lead to many rooms and halls.

Some gnomes make small homes in tree trunks. Others dig burrows.

In Sweden, some families set out rice pudding for gnomes on Christmas Eve.

Gnome Eggs help gnomes stay hidden. They are located on mountains or deep in the woods. Even so, people sometimes find Gnome Eggs. Some people even go inside. They visit the magical world where gnomes live.

Other gnomes live near homes or farms. They help the people who live there. But people must be careful. If they don't take good care of their homes or animals, gnomes could punish them. In Scandinavia, gnomes are said to love tradition. They get mad if people make too many changes.

All stories of gnomes are a little different. Each story is shaped by the people telling it. And people continue to tell new stories.

FUN FACT
Legends say setting out a bowl of porridge for gnomes could make them happy.

GOBLIN

Sneaky Spirit

A man walks through the forest alone. It is a moonless night. The sky is very dark. If the man isn't careful, he could get lost.

Suddenly, the man sees a light in the distance. It seems to move. He tries to walk toward the light. But it keeps moving away. The man follows the light as it flashes and dances. At last, he gets close enough to see what it is. The light comes from a candle. A small creature holds it. The creature is a goblin!

The goblin leads the man to a cliff. Then it winks at him and blows the candle out. The man is left in the dark.

FUN FACT
Sometimes a group of goblins dance together. The dance makes people fall asleep.

Several legends tell of lights or creatures that make people get lost.

Goblins are known for their creepy looks and tricky behavior.

Goblins Around the World

Goblins appear in stories from around the world. Some legends are very old. They tell of sneaky spirits. But the creatures are not always bad. For example, dokkaebi appear in many Korean folktales. Some of these stories are more than 1,000 years old. Dokkaebi often want to meet people or play games. But they can also cause disease or start fires.

Buildings in ancient Korea often had pictures of dokkaebi on their roof tiles.

In Japan, people told legends of the tengu. These spirits live in mountains. They have wings like birds. They also have long beaks or large noses.

In early stories, tengu were evil. They kidnapped children. Later, the stories became funnier and less scary.

Mischievous spirits also appear in folktales from North America. The legends vary depending on the Indigenous nation. Each group has its own stories.

Algonquin legends tell of small people who live in the forest. These beings are usually not dangerous. But in Wampanoag legends, the creatures can hurt or kidnap people.

Some tengu have beaks and claws like birds.

In Europe, goblin stories were told as early as the 1300s. Many stories spread throughout England, Ireland, and Wales. Others came from Denmark or Germany. Goblins in these Western legends were more likely to behave badly. Some spirits were just naughty. Others were said to be evil. But all used magic to play tricks.

Goblin Traits

A goblin's appearance can vary depending on the story. Tengu have wings. Dokkaebi have long teeth and claws. Sometimes they have horns, too.

In stories from Europe, goblins are often similar to fairies. In fact, people sometimes used the terms interchangeably. For example, Welsh people told stories of fairies that lived underground. They called these creatures "coblynau." This name sounds a little bit like the word *goblin*.

Many goblins have small bodies. They often look very ugly. Their ears and noses tend to be quite large. They may also have huge mouths and bulging eyes. A few goblins are covered in hair.

Depending on the story, goblins may also be called hobgoblins or bugbears.

Story Spotlight

Welsh legends say coblynau live in tunnels and mines. These creatures stand about 18 inches (46 cm) tall. Their name means "knockers" or "thumpers." Usually, coblynau are helpful. They tap on walls to show miners where to find ore. But miners must watch out. If they insult a coblynau, it may throw rocks at them. Germany has stories of similar creatures. One creature, called a kobold, tends to be more mischievous. Kobolds often trick or bother miners. But they sometimes help people.

Countries around the world have legends of creatures dwelling in mines.

Some goblins are invisible. These goblins are similar to ghosts. They can't be seen. But they can make sounds and throw things. These goblins often live in or near houses. But they sometimes live in swamps or forests. Stories warn travelers to watch out. Meeting a goblin could be very dangerous.

FUN FACT

In one legend, a goblin lives in a castle. She can turn into ivy and grow on the walls.

Stories about goblins often warn people to stay away from them.

Some types of goblins can cast spells and do magic.

Many goblins have magical powers. Some can shape-shift. They can make themselves look like people or animals. Other goblins can predict when people will die.

Goblins often use these powers to trick or scare people. In many stories, goblins make loud noises. Some goblins bang on pots and pans. Others screech and rattle windows or doors.

FUN FACT
Some goblins have the power to send people flying through the air.

Goblin Behavior

Goblins tend to be mischievous. They like to play pranks on people. These tricks confuse or annoy people. But they usually don't hurt anyone. For example, goblins may move people's furniture at night. They may also take or hide people's belongings. The people wake up to a surprise.

In many stories, goblins have bad tempers. They get angry easily.

In some German folktales, goblin-like creatures called kobolds help in people's homes.

In a few stories, goblins are meaner. These goblins try to make people get lost. They lure people deep into a forest or swamp. Some of those people never return. And a few goblins are said to hurt or kidnap people.

However, not all goblins are bad. Some will help people do chores. But first, people need to give them something. For example, people can give the goblins food. Or they can light a fire for heat. In return, the goblins may help care for their home or farm.

Other goblins help miners. Some knock on the rock to show miners good places to dig. Others warn miners of danger. If something bad is about to happen, the goblins tap the mine's wall three times. In fact, some stories even say goblins can be good luck.

FUN FACT

Some goblins punish naughty children. But they bring gifts for children who behave well.

KRAKEN

Terror at Sea

A group of fishermen haul in their heavy nets. Suddenly, a dark shape moves under the boats. It's the kraken!

Huge tentacles shoot up out of the water. They grab one of the boats. They drag it under the waves. The other fishermen are terrified. They try to escape.

The kraken is said to lurk deep in the ocean.

According to legends, the kraken can pull any ship underwater.

The kraken slips back underwater. But it makes a whirlpool. It's hard for the ships to get away from the swirling water. One boat is pulled down with the beast. The other boats get home safely.

FUN FACT
In some stories, the kraken can control the weather.

Spreading the Legend

The kraken is a legendary beast. It is said to live in the northern Atlantic Ocean. These waters are between Norway and Greenland.

Long ago, people in these areas used long boats to travel and fish. Sailors brought stories back to shore. They told of a huge beast with many arms. Sailors said the beast lived deep underwater. But sometimes it came up to the surface. It attacked boats. Then it sank back down.

The kraken is said to live in cold waters near the coast of Norway.

Story Spotlight

Norway has a long coastline. Its people sailed to distant lands. They fished for food. The sea was important to them. This is clear in their legends, including tales of the kraken. In legends, good fishing is a sign the kraken is nearby. The creature scares fish into coming up to the water's surface.

Cod is one of the top kinds of fish caught in Norway.

Looks and Behavior

A Scandinavian writer described the kraken in 1755. He gathered tales about the beast. He shared what he learned. He said the kraken was the biggest sea monster on Earth. He said it was round and flat. And it had many arms. The writer said the kraken's arms stretched as tall as a ship's mast.

The writer explained how the kraken hunted. He said its poop floated on the water. The smell attracted many fish. The kraken came up to eat them.

Some illustrations show the kraken grabbing boats.

Story Spotlight

The kraken is not the only dangerous creature that sailors might face. A similar monster called Scylla appears in Greek myths. This monster has six heads. It sits on the coast. It eats sailors who come too close. Greek myths also tell of a sea monster that lives in a whirlpool. This monster's name is Charybdis. Together, the two monsters trap and eat many sailors.

The kraken looks similar to a giant octopus.

An Explanation?

In the 1850s, scientists began learning more about the giant squid. This animal lives deep underwater. But giant squid sometimes wash up on beaches after they die. By studying the bodies, scientists can learn about this mysterious animal. They realized the kraken might be based on the giant squid.

The giant squid lives in oceans around the world. It has two tentacles and eight arms. It may grow up to 50 feet (15 m) long. A giant squid's arms are covered in suction cups. These suction cups have sharp edges. The squid can use them to grab or fight other animals.

Giant squid hunt many animals, including fish, jellyfish, and other squid.

Giant squid have been known to fight animals as big as whales.

Long ago, sailors could have seen giant squid. They could have created tales of the kraken to explain what they saw.

The colossal squid may be even bigger than the giant squid. But it didn't inspire the kraken. The colossal squid lives in a different part of the world. It is found only in the waters near Antarctica.

MERMAID

Under the Sea

When morning comes, the mermaid smiles. She plans her day. First, she will pick a bouquet of beautiful sea anemones. Then, she will play with the dolphins. The coral reef is also fun to visit. She loves to see the dazzling colors and shapes.

Mermaids spend most of their time deep below the water's surface.

Mermaids may bring humans to shore to save them from drowning.

But first, the mermaid swims above the waves and looks around. She does this every morning. Today, she sees a big ship. Then she notices a boy in the water. He is sinking!

Normally, the mermaid hides from humans. Yet she knows she must help. After saving the boy, she will disappear once again.

FUN FACT
In some stories, mermaids are immortal. This means they can live forever.

History of Mermaids

The word *mermaid* comes from two old words. *Mere* means "sea," and *maid* means "girl." Put together, *mermaid* means "girl of the sea." The words *mermen* and *merfolk* also describe the mythical creatures. *Mermen* describes males, and *merfolk* describes all genders.

In stories, Oannes was the first merman. This ancient god was half man and half fish. The goddess Atargatis was the first mermaid. She was half woman and half fish.

Greek myths include many tales of merfolk. The god Triton was a merman. He used a trident to control the sea. A trident is a spear with three points.

Myths also told of sirens. A siren was half woman and half bird. In later stories, sirens looked like mermaids. They inspired many mermaid tales.

FUN FACT

The *Odyssey* is a long Greek poem from the 700s BCE. It was the first story to mention sirens.

Atargatis appears on this ancient coin from Greece.

A statue in Saint Petersburg, Russia, shows Triton battling a dragon.

In 1836, Hans Christian Andersen wrote *The Little Mermaid*. In this tale, a mermaid wants to become human. Many movies are based on this popular story.

Today, most stories about mermaids are fictional. In the past, however, more people believed in mermaids. Oceans are huge and mysterious. People wondered what lived in the water. They used stories of mermaids to explain it. For example, the explorer Christopher Columbus claimed he saw a mermaid. However, he probably saw a manatee or a dugong. These sea animals have large tails. Scientists think legends of mermaids may be based on these animals.

FUN FACT

In 2013, a TV channel made a fake news show about mermaids. Afterwards, some people were confused. They thought mermaids might be real.

Swimming manatees may look similar to mermaids.

Story Spotlight

Some people dress up as mermaids for their jobs. They wear tails made from fabric or silicone. They perform in shows at theme parks or aquariums. They swim and dive for audiences. Professional mermaids must be able to swim well. They need to hold their breath for a long time. And their tails can weigh as much as 45 pounds (20 kg).

A professional mermaid performs in a show in China.

Mermaid Appearance

A mermaid is human from the waist up. From the waist down, she is a fish. She has a large, shiny tail that is covered in scales. These scales can be many colors.

Most mermaids are beautiful. They have long, flowing hair. Sometimes, they wear shells or coral. Mermaids collect these items as jewelry. In many stories, mermaids carry a mirror and comb. They are often vain. They like to look at their reflections. They also like to brush their hair.

In stories, mermaids live alongside other sea creatures.

Some mermaids have brightly colored hair, skin, and eyes.

Mermen are similar to mermaids. They also have long hair. Some have beards, too. Most mermen are large and strong.

The appearance of mermaids depends on the story. In Irish myths, mermaids and mermen are called merrows. Female merrows have pale skin and dark eyes. A male merrow has green skin, hair, and teeth. He also has webbed fingers.

FUN FACT
Japanese folklore tells of mermaid-like creatures called kappa. The kappa is a water spirit. It has an ape-like face and a turtle-like shell.

Mermaid Behavior

Mermaids make their homes in the ocean. Some live alone in sea caves. Others live in underwater kingdoms. They belong to a community of merfolk.

Mermaids are musical creatures. They love to sing. Some mermaids use their singing to trick humans. Sirens sing magical songs to attract sailors. The sailors follow the music. Then, the sirens drown them in the water.

Mermaids take breaks from swimming by sitting on rocks.

Sirens call out to a group of sailors.

Other mermaids are kind. They are interested in humans. Some help humans who are in danger. However, mermaids can also be shy. They often hide from humans.

In European folklore, selkies are similar to mermaids. When selkies are in the water, they look like seals. But on land, they lose their seal skin. They become humans. They fall in love and have families. Soon, however, they miss the water. If a selkie's husband finds the seal skin, he hides it. Otherwise, the selkie will put it on. She will become a seal and return to the sea.

FUN FACT

Mami Wata is a spirit in African myths. She often takes the form of a mermaid. She can bring both bad and good luck.

OGRE

Danger in the Woods

Seven brothers are lost in the woods. They know an ogre lives nearby. So, they need somewhere safe to spend the night. The brothers walk and walk. Finally, they see a cabin.

The boys knock on the door. A woman lets them inside. But she warns them. Her husband is an ogre. And he will be back soon.

Suddenly, the boys hear heavy footsteps outside the door. It's the ogre!

Most ogres have big heads and hairy bodies.

Ogres often carry large clubs or other weapons.

The boys hide under the bed, but the ogre finds them. He grabs the boys and tries to eat them. But his wife convinces him to wait until morning. While he sleeps, the boys creep outside and run away.

FUN FACT
Many ogres live alone. But some have families.

Ogres Around the World

The history of ogres goes back many years. In ancient Italy, people had a god called Orcus. Many people feared him. His body was large and hairy. Legends said he killed and ate people.

Over time, people told stories of monsters with similar traits. These creatures were often called ogres. Like Orcus, they were big, mean, and ugly.

Many cultures have stories of ogres. Oni appear in folktales from Japan. These ogres are known for being scary and evil. Their bodies are often big and strong.

A sculpture at the Park of the Monsters in Italy shows Orcus's huge mouth.

Statues of oni or similar creatures called nio often decorate temples.

In Papua New Guinea, stories tell of origorúsos. These ogres walk on four legs. They live underground or in trees. But they raid villages. Their huge mouths can swallow people whole.

Other tales come from Europe. In the late 1600s, a French man wrote a book of children's stories. The book was called *Tales of Mother Goose*. It was based on old folktales. It used the word *ogre* for monsters that ate people.

The stories became very popular in Europe. Tales about ogres continued to spread. By the 1700s, legends of ogres were common in Great Britain. These creatures were said to eat children. The stories warned children not to go far from home.

FUN FACT
An origorúso has huge ears. It can use them as a blanket.

Ogre Traits

Ogres are strong and tall. They are similar to giants. But ogres tend to be uglier. They often have green or blue skin. Their bodies may be covered in hair. Many ogres have hooked noses, too.

In Japan, oni have horns. Their skin is often pink, red, or blue. Oni have three toes on each foot. Some oni have three eyes as well.

In England, legends said many scary ogres roamed the land. Some had two or three heads. One was a giant who carried a large bag. He grabbed children and stuffed them inside. Then he ate them.

Ogres have big appetites. They can eat huge amounts of food. And they love to eat raw meat. Ogres have large mouths and long, sharp teeth. In addition, ogres have a strong sense of smell. They can tell if people or animals are nearby.

Some ogres have special powers. For example, some ogres can shape-shift. They can change into different kinds of animals. In one story, an ogre turns into a lion to attack. But then the ogre gets tricked into turning into a mouse. A cat eats it.

> **FUN FACT**
> One story tells of an ogre with feathers. The feathers are magical. They can cure sickness.

A female ogre is called an ogress.

Some ogres can do magic.

Ogre Behavior

In most stories, ogres are mean monsters. They attack homes and villages. Ogres steal and eat livestock. But their main source of food is people. In many stories, ogres chase and catch children. Ogres may also try to trap people or keep them as prisoners.

Ogres often live in lonely places. Some make their homes in the woods. Others live in mountains and caves. Most ogres are not

A fountain in Switzerland shows an ogre eating children.

Ogres live in swamps or other dark places.

very smart. People can trick them and escape. For example, people can use disguises. The ogres get confused. They attack or eat the wrong things.

Other ogres are more intelligent. These ogres can be rich and powerful. They may live in huge houses or castles. But they still tend to be tricky and mean.

FUN FACT
One ogre had magic boots. Anyone who wore them could go 21 miles (34 km) in one step.

Some ogres are greedy. They hoard treasure. Other ogres capture people. However, people can outsmart them and get away. In several stories, people challenge an ogre to a contest. If the ogre loses, the people can go free.

In rare cases, ogres can be friendly. They live with people or marry humans. A few stories are even funny. Stories about ogres continue to change. People keep creating new versions.

One famous story tells of a cat that outsmarts an ogre.

Story Spotlight

In the Shrek series, the main character is an ogre. Shrek lives in a swamp. He takes mud showers and eats bugs. Shrek likes being alone. But unlike other ogres, Shrek doesn't eat people. In fact, he has a kind heart. Shrek helps a princess named Fiona. Because of a curse, she turns into an ogre every night. Shrek and Fiona fall in love. She stays an ogre and marries him.

Shrek is an ogre with bright-green skin. He is the main character of several movies.

PEGASUS

Flying High

A hero walks through the forest. He is looking for Pegasus. He finds the white horse by a small pond. Its wings shine in the sun.

The hero needs to defeat a monster. He asks Pegasus to help. Pegasus nods. It lets the hero climb onto its back.

The winged horse starts running. Then it leaps into the air. The hero and the horse soar through the sky. They fly off to fight the monster.

A statue in Austria's Mirabella Gardens shows Pegasus leaping.

Pegasus is the name of one particular horse in Greek myths. But some people use the word *pegasus* for any horse with wings.

History of Pegasus

Pegasus is a magical horse with wings. It comes from Greek mythology. Pegasus has a white coat. Its mane and tail are white, too.

Pegasus was related to Medusa. She was a monster with snakes for hair. Medusa had the power to turn anyone who looked at her into stone. Pegasus was born from her blood when a hero killed her.

In art and stories, Pegasus is often a symbol of strength and speed. The winged horse can fly high in the sky. It can run very fast on the ground. Pegasus can also create springs by stomping its hoof. Springs are places where water bubbles up from underground.

FUN FACT

Pegasus's father was Poseidon, the Greek god of the sea.

The name *Pegasus* may mean "of the spring" or "sprung forth."

Story Spotlight

One famous spring supposedly made by Pegasus is on Mount Helicon. This spring's water is said to help poets be creative. In some legends, this spring is also associated with the Muses. These Greek goddesses were daughters of Zeus. They helped people make art. Some stories said Pegasus belonged to the Muses, too.

Legends say some springs give power to people who drink or bathe in their water.

Adventures

At first, Pegasus was wild and free. Later, a hero tamed it. The hero's name was Bellerophon. He and Pegasus had many adventures. Pegasus helped Bellerophon win fights. In one fight, the hero killed the Chimera. This monster had

Bellerophon rode Pegasus to defeat the Chimera. This dangerous monster was part lion, part goat, and part snake.

Story Spotlight

Several constellations get their names from Greek myths. One constellation is named after Pegasus. In Greece, these stars first appear at the end of summer. This marks the beginning of thunderstorm season. According to legend, the gods placed Pegasus in the stars. This was a reward for the winged horse's help.

three heads. It could also breathe fire. Bellerophon used Pegasus to fly above this monster and kill it.

After a while, however, Bellerophon became too proud. He tried flying on Pegasus to Mount Olympus. This was where the gods lived. The gods got angry. They sent a fly to bite Pegasus.

The horse bucked Bellerophon. He fell back to the earth. But Pegasus stayed with the gods. It carried lightning and thunder for Zeus, the rule of the Greek gods. Some stories say Pegasus helped the goddess Eos bring the dawn.

In the constellation Pegasus, a box represents the horse's body. Lines show the head and legs.

Horses in Legends

In ancient Greece, horses were valuable. They had many uses. People used them to hunt, fight, and travel. Horses also cost a lot. Owning one was a sign of status. Having a horse showed that someone was rich or important.

People often create myths about things they value. Horses were important to many cultures. So, horses appeared in the stories they told. For example, in Korea and China, legends tell of a winged horse. It is called the Chollima. It is said to be too fast for any human to ride.

Many cultures have art and stories about winged horses.

Several magical horses appear in Greek myths. Pegasus is one of them. Others are said to pull chariots for the gods. For example, the god Ares has four magical horses. They can breathe fire. The god Poseidon has four hippocamps. These creatures are half horse and half fish.

A hippocamp has the upper body of a horse. Its lower half is a fish.

Pegasus appears on many coins from ancient Greece.

PHOENIX

From the Ashes

The sun is rising. The phoenix soars across the sky. Its feathers shine with bright colors. The phoenix lands in its nest. Then it bursts into flames. Branches crackle and snap as the fire grows.

Finally, the fire dies down. Only a pile of ash is left. But the phoenix is not dead. Instead, it is reborn. The phoenix rises from the ashes.

The phoenix's eyes and feathers can glow like fire.

Some stories say the phoenix is invincible. This means it cannot be killed or hurt.

Looks and Behavior

Stories of the phoenix began in ancient times. The legends tell of a magical bird that can live forever. The bird has beautiful feathers. They are often red, orange, and gold. They can be purple, too. Some stories say the bird looks like an eagle. Others say it is like a peacock.

FUN FACT
Some stories say the phoenix's eyes are like blue gems.

Like a peacock, a phoenix can have a long tail.

Each time the phoenix burns, it becomes young again.

There is only one phoenix. But every 500 years, it sets itself on fire to be born again. When the phoenix is about to die, it builds a nest from wood and spices. Then the bird sits down. It begins to sing. The song is very beautiful. After the song ends, the nest catches fire. The phoenix burns, and then it comes back to life.

FUN FACT
In some stories, the phoenix makes its nest in a palm tree. In others, it flies to a temple for the god of the sun.

Spreading the Legend

The phoenix appears in Greek myths. But those stories are based on earlier tales from Egypt. The Egyptians told stories of a bird called the Bennu. This bird was said to look like a heron. Like the sun, it rose each morning to be reborn. Stories also said the Bennu helped create the world.

Later, a Greek historian wrote these stories down. The stories spread around the world. Other cultures have similar legends. Many are about hope and rebirth.

The Bennu appears in the Book of the Dead. This book was written in ancient Egypt.

Story Spotlight

Magical birds appear in the folktales of many different countries. Chinese legends tell of the feng huang. Like a phoenix, this bird is immortal. People rarely see it. But when they do, it's a sign of peace and good luck. Russian folktales tell of the firebird. It has magical feathers. Stories of the firebird inspired a famous ballet.

Today, the phoenix appears in art and stories from around the world. As the legends about it spread, people added new details. In some stories, the phoenix can change sizes. In others, its tears have the power to heal.

In China, the feng huang often decorates palaces and temples.

A phoenix decorates a stained-glass window in a church in Belgium.

An Explanation?

People often create myths to explain things they don't fully understand. What happens after death is a common topic. For example, the phoenix is used as a symbol in several myths and religions. It often represents rebirth.

Legends may also be based on fossils. People find the bones of ancient animals. They guess what those animals looked like.

Story Spotlight

In the 1900s, scientists found the bones of a huge heron. They named it the Bennu heron, after the mythical Bennu bird. The Bennu heron is extinct. The bones scientists found are thousands of years old. Scientists studied the bones. They think the bird grew more than 6.5 feet (2 m) tall. The Goliath heron is the largest heron alive today. It's almost 5 feet (1.5 m) tall.

Long ago, a huge kind of heron lived in the Middle East. People may have found this bird's bones. They may have told legends about the phoenix to explain the bones.

Fossils can give people a general sense of what animals looked like.

A Narrow Escape

The sailors hear a loud boom. Then their ship rocks to one side. A sea serpent is attacking!

The captain spins the ship's wheel. But he can't turn fast enough. The sea serpent strikes again. Huge waves splash onto the deck. Soon, the ship will sink.

Some sea serpents wrap their bodies around ships to sink them.

However, the crew is in luck. A gust of wind blows. It fills the sails. The ship races away. For now, the crew is safe.

Sea serpents and other monsters decorate an old map of northern Europe.

Legends Around the World

Many cultures tell stories of sea monsters. These creatures often look like huge snakes or dragons. Sea serpents have long, thin bodies. A few have wings or legs. Many sea serpents have sharp teeth and spikes on their backs.

Tales of sea serpents are hundreds of years old. Some tales come from Europe. These stories began in Scandinavia. Sailors told of terrifying monsters. They said the beasts sank ships.

Sea serpents are said to be fast, powerful swimmers.

Nagas can be found near rivers, lakes, oceans, or other bodies of water.

Other stories come from Asia. For example, Japanese folklore tells of a mighty dragon. He is the god of the sea. He has great power. He controls the tides. Nagas are snake-like creatures that appear in the folklore of several cultures. Nagas can be dangerous. But sometimes they are helpful. For example, some nagas guard treasure.

Inuit folklore warns of dangerous sea snakes. These snakes can grow up to 15 feet (4.5 m) long. They grab people off docks. They pull people into the water.

FUN FACT
One story tells of a huge sea serpent. It could wrap around the whole world.

Looks and Behavior

In the 1500s, a Swedish writer made books and maps. They told about Scandinavia. Some had stories and drawings of sea serpents. The writer said sea serpents were huge. They could grow 200 feet (61 m) long. They had black scales and bright-red eyes. They were dangerous, too. At night, they hunted for food. Sometimes, sea serpents ate animals. Other times, they attacked ships and ate sailors.

FUN FACT
Some sea serpents are shown with manes like lions.

Old illustrations often show sea monsters chasing ships.

Story Spotlight

Stories from Canada say a mysterious creature lives in Okanagan Lake. Some stories were spread by settlers. They called the creature Ogopogo. They said it had a long body. Depending on the story, its head looked like a horse, a snake, or a sheep. Indigenous people have their own legends about the lake. They say a water spirit lives there. This spirit may appear as a creature with a horse's head and a deer's antlers.

The monster Ogopogo is usually said to have green or black skin.

An Explanation?

Some snakes live in warm ocean waters. But legends say sea serpents live in cold places. So, scientists think sea serpents may be based on other animals. For example, people may have seen oarfish. These fish are long and flat. They usually swim deep underwater. But sometimes they come near the surface.

FUN FACT
Oarfish are harmless to humans. They eat fish and tiny sea creatures.

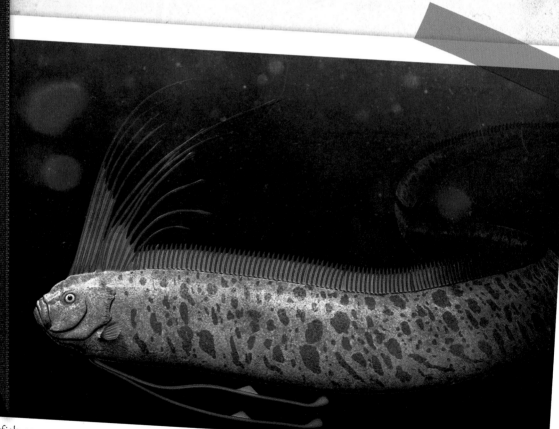

Oarfish can grow up to 36 feet (11 m) long.

Basking sharks often swim near the surface with their mouths open.

People may also have seen basking sharks. These sharks have huge mouths. If threatened, basking sharks sometimes attack boats.

FUN FACT
Basking sharks can grow 40 feet (12 m) long.

TROLL

Finding Food

Three trolls march through a pine forest under the stars. Their heads reach the treetops. Rabbits and squirrels scurry away from the trolls' feet. They do not want to be crushed.

The troll in front has one yellow eye that is as big as a bicycle wheel. The eye sits in the middle of his forehead. It lights up the path like a flashlight. The other two trolls have empty spaces instead of eyes.

Some forest trolls blend in with the trees around them.

Many trolls have bad eyesight. Instead, they rely on their noses to find food.

The troll in front is the leader. The second troll holds on to the leader's shoulder. And the third troll holds on to the tail of the second. All three sniff the path ahead. They move faster and faster to catch the humans they smell.

History of Trolls

People have told stories of trolls for thousands of years. Many of these stories started in Norway and other Scandinavian countries. Trolls first appeared in stories of Norse gods such as Odin and Thor. These gods protected the world from creatures called frost giants. The first frost giant was Ymir. He gave birth to trolls out of his feet.

In Norse folklore, trolls are evil. They are dangerous creatures that hate humans. According to legend, trolls live in forests, mountains, oceans, and lakes. At night, they roam below the northern lights.

The Scandinavian countries were home to many storytellers. They told stories on mountain farms and by the sea. In the winter, they gathered around fires. Troll stories were entertaining and helpful. The stories warned people of danger. Listeners learned that they needed to be smart to survive. Strangers, seas, and dark places could lead them to trolls.

In the 1840s, two friends wrote down troll stories. Their names were Peter Christen Asbjornsen and Jorgen Moe.

Troll figurines are popular in Scandinavian countries.

Story Spotlight

In many countries, troll dolls are popular children's toys. These small dolls have short arms and legs. Their hair tends to be very bright colors. It sticks straight up into the air. Troll dolls were first made in Denmark in the 1950s. The dolls are meant to bring good luck.

They collected Norse folklore. Without them, many troll stories could have been lost.

Trolls continue to fascinate people today. Trolls appear in many TV shows, movies, and books.

The first troll dolls were made of wood. Today, they're made from plastic.

Types of Trolls

In Norse mythology, trolls come in many shapes and sizes. Most trolls are huge. However, they can also be tiny. Some have barnacles on their backs. Others have tails. Older trolls often have bushes growing in their hair.

A troll's appearance depends on the type of troll. Trolls are grouped into types based on where they live.

FUN FACT
Huldra trolls use magic to make themselves beautiful. Then they trick humans into marrying them.

In some stories, trolls interact with fairies and other mythical creatures.

A bridge troll may catch and eat people who cross above it.

Mountain trolls are one example. These huge trolls are as solid as rock. One mountain troll can have more than 12 heads. The heads often scream and bite at humans.

Water trolls are another type. They live in lakes, rivers, and wells. These trolls have wet, slimy hands. Many water trolls can change their shape. Ocean trolls are a type of water troll. They have mouths as big as hay wagons. These trolls are cloaked in seaweed and shells. They also have powerful fingers for grabbing humans.

Some trolls live below bridges. They are known for being lumpy and ugly. Other trolls live in forests. Forest trolls are hairy and smelly. They are filled with so much dirt that plants grow on them.

FUN FACT
Bridge trolls were made famous in the tale "The Three Billy Goats Gruff."

Troll Behavior

According to legend, trolls are at war with humans. They use their powers to hurt people. For example, mountain trolls throw rocks. This can cause avalanches. Lake trolls can change into boats. They lure people into the water and drown them. Ocean trolls scare fishers with their huge, open mouths.

Trolls have a strong sense of smell. This helps them catch and eat humans. Forest trolls are especially good at this task. They cook humans in soups. The trolls' long noses are perfect for stirring.

Trolls may use their ugly appearance to scare humans.

Some trolls are fierce fighters. They are very strong.

Trolls are greedy creatures. They fill their caves with gold and gems. Some trolls cast spells. They can turn humans into animals such as bears. Trolls use their magic to carry people to their castles.

However, trolls have many weaknesses. The sound of church bells scares them. And sunlight turns them to stone. Most trolls are not intelligent. Humans can often escape trolls by outsmarting them.

FUN FACT
In some stories, fishers throw dirt from cemeteries at ocean trolls. This scares the trolls away.

UNICORN

Hard to Catch

A unicorn rests deep in the forest. He wakes up to a sunny day. He drinks from a flowing stream. A soft breeze blows his mane. Around him, birds tweet. Flowers grow in the sun.

The unicorn's ears flicker. Horse hooves pound against the ground. Voices call out. The hunters have returned. They want to capture the mysterious unicorn. Nobody has ever caught a unicorn. But the hunters are determined. They will not give up.

In many stories, unicorns are rare creatures that are hard to capture.

Some unicorns live alone. Others have families.

The unicorn gallops through the trees. He knows the forest well. He hides in a cave until the hunters ride away. Then the unicorn comes out. He stays very quiet in case the hunters return.

FUN FACT
The unicorn is the national animal of Scotland. It's seen as a symbol of independence.

History of Unicorns

People have told stories about unicorns for many years. The stories come from all over the world. Unicorns were first mentioned in writing around 2700 BCE. These stories came from Asia.

In the 300s BCE, a Greek historian wrote about unicorns. His name was Ctesias. He had heard of the creature from Indian travelers. The travelers claimed they had seen unicorns. However, they most likely saw a rhinoceros.

In the Middle Ages, an artist created the Unicorn Tapestries. The tapestries, or wall hangings, tell a story. Pictures on the cloth show

> **FUN FACT**
> In the 1200s CE, explorer Marco Polo claimed to see a unicorn. He described it as an ugly beast.

The Indian rhinoceros lives in northern India and Nepal. Unlike some other rhinos, it has just one horn.

Today, the Unicorn Tapestries hang in an art museum in New York.

men hunting a unicorn. In the same period, authors wrote books about mythical creatures. These books were called bestiaries. Many bestiaries included descriptions of unicorns. Writers described how unicorns looked and behaved. They thought the creatures had magical powers.

Unicorn Appearance

The unicorn is best known for the horn on its forehead. In fact, that's where the creature gets its name. In Latin, *uni* means "one." *Cornu* means "horn." These words blend together to make the word *unicorn*.

Today, unicorns are usually described as white horses with long, spiral-shaped horns. In many early stories, however, the unicorn has the body of a goat. On its head is a short, colorful horn.

A unicorn's appearance can vary depending on the story. Ctesias described unicorns as large and white. He said their horns were red, black, and white. He also said unicorns had purple heads and blue

A brown unicorn was featured in a bestiary from the 1200s CE.

A kylin's scales are often brightly colored.

eyes. Other stories say unicorns can be black, brown, or golden. Many unicorns have traits of other animals. They may have a lion's tail or a goat's beard.

Several countries have their own unicorn myths. For example, the Chinese unicorn is called a kylin. The kylin has the body of a deer and the head of a dragon. It is covered in fish-like scales. Other Asian countries have stories of similar creatures.

Persian legends tell of the karkadann. This creature looks like a buffalo. But each of its feet has three hooves. It also has a horn of gold.

FUN FACT
Some unicorns have wings. These creatures are sometimes called alicorns. A unicorn's horn may be called an alicorn as well.

Unicorn Behavior

According to legend, unicorns live in forests. They feed on grass and moss. Most unicorns live in quiet solitude. Humans rarely see them. However, several stories say that unicorns are drawn to beautiful maidens. These young girls are allowed to come close or pet them.

In most myths, unicorns are gentle creatures. They are wise and kind. Asian unicorns show care for all living things. They walk very softly. They do not want to hurt insects or blades of grass. These unicorns are signs of power and peace.

In some myths, young girls are able to calm wild unicorns.

Because they are gentle and kind, unicorns are signs of goodness or honor in many stories.

However, unicorns can also be fierce and strong. In fact, the karkadann is a brave warrior. It fights animals such as elephants. The karkadann can even change the shape of its body.

FUN FACT

In some stories, unicorns and lions are enemies. They fight one another in battles.

Unicorns have magical powers. Their horns have the power to heal. For example, a unicorn horn can work against poison. The unicorn touches its horn to water. This makes the water safe to drink. Unicorns often use their powers to help animals and humans.

Because of these powers, people in stories often hunt unicorns. However, unicorns are hard to catch. They usually get away. But in some stories, hunters use a maiden to lure a unicorn. Then they kill the unicorn. They make medicine from its horn.

In the Middle Ages, many people believed unicorns were real. Some people thought unicorn horns could cure illness. Today, few people believe in unicorns. But stories of unicorns remain popular.

A unicorn uses its horn to do magic.

Story Spotlight

In the Middle Ages, some people claimed to sell unicorn horns. However, these horns were fake. Most came from narwhals. A narwhal is a type of whale. A long tooth sticks out of a male narwhal's mouth. This tooth can grow up to 10 feet (3.0 m) long. It has a spiral shape. People hunted narwhals and sold their teeth as unicorn horns. Queen Elizabeth I of England owned one of these horns. It cost as much as a castle.

Narwhals are sometimes called the unicorns of the sea. They live in Arctic waters.

VAMPIRE

Thirsty for Blood

When night falls, the castle goes dark. In the castle's tallest tower, a coffin opens. The vampire inside slowly opens his eyes. He has been sleeping for a long time. Now he is thirsty. He needs blood to drink.

The vampire changes into his bat form and flies out the window. Soon, he smells blood. He turns back into his human form. He floats to the ground.

The vampire catches his prey with lightning speed. He bites the victim's throat with his sharp fangs. Then he sucks the victim's blood. Feeling satisfied, he turns back into a bat. He flies until sunrise.

Legends say that vampires sleep in coffins or other dark places.

Vampires may disguise themselves as bats while hunting.

History of Vampires

Vampires are mythical creatures. Most vampires are humans who have died and come back to life. In stories, vampires leave their graves at night. They suck the blood of humans and animals.

Vampire stories have existed for thousands of years. In many ancient stories, vampires

FUN FACT
Long ago, humans used vampire stories to explain natural events. For example, some people said vampires caused illness.

MORT DU CHOLERA
Certifie par nous Dochu...

Vampires are undead. That means they have come back from the grave.

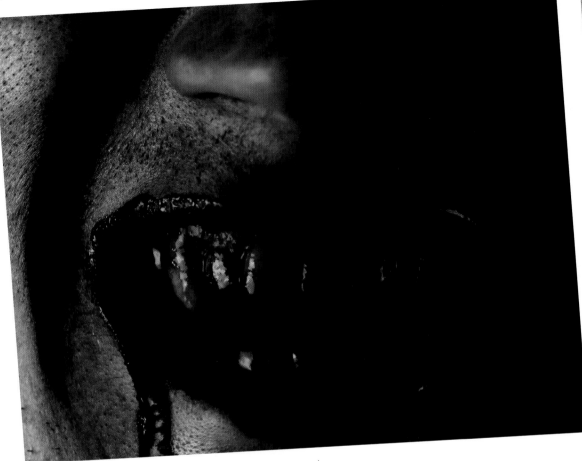

If vampires don't drink enough blood, they become weak.

were not humans. They were evil spirits. This version of the myth may have come from Egypt or Greece.

Other legends of vampires began in Eastern Europe. People in small villages often told stories of these bloodsucking creatures. In Romania, vampires were called strigoi. Some strigoi were living humans. Others became vampires after they died.

In early stories, vampires were evil and creepy. These early vampires were not pale. Their skin was slightly red. This was because they were filled with blood.

In the 1700s and 1800s, the image of the vampire began to change. Vampires began to appear in many books and plays. These vampires had pale skin and slick, black hair. They often wore long capes. And many of them were rich and handsome.

In more recent stories, humans sometimes fall in love with handsome vampires.

Story Spotlight

One of the most famous vampires is Count Dracula. He is from the book *Dracula*. This book came out in 1897. It tells the story of a count in Transylvania who kills people and drinks their blood. A movie based on this book was made in 1931. This film helped make vampires more popular.

The castle in the movie *Dracula* is based on Bran Castle in Romania.

Vampire Appearance

Vampires can come in many shapes and sizes. Some vampires look similar to humans. For example, the strigoi have some human features. They have red hair and blue eyes. Unlike humans, however, strigoi have two hearts. One of the hearts never dies.

Other vampires don't look like humans at all. For example, some legends say vampires have no bones. These vampires look like

FUN FACT
In many stories, vampires don't have shadows or reflections. If vampires look in a mirror, they cannot see themselves.

Like vampires, bats are nocturnal. A few types of bats even eat blood.

A vampire quickly returns to its human shape before drinking blood.

shapeless bags of blood. If the vampire lives for 40 days, it changes. The vampire gains bones and a body.

Many vampires have the ability to shape-shift into other forms. Their most common form is a bat. But they can also turn into wolves, rats, and other animals. As a result, it is difficult for humans to spot vampires.

Vampires can range from being very beautiful to extremely ugly. However, vampires do have a few things in common. Vampires need blood to stay alive. The blood can come from an animal or a human. Many vampires have sharp fangs. Vampires use their fangs to bite the neck or throat. Some stories say that when a vampire bites a human, that human turns into a vampire, too.

Vampire Behavior

According to folklore, vampires are immortal. They can live forever. Some vampires live alone. But others live in groups. A group of vampires is called a coven or clan.

Vampires may hunt alone or in groups.

Most vampires sleep during the day. They prefer tight, dark places such as coffins. At night, vampires come out to hunt.

Vampires have sharp hearing and a strong sense of smell. They can see in the dark. And they have super strength and speed. Vampires can climb walls and make large jumps. As a result, humans rarely see vampires coming until it's too late.

In some stories, people fight against vampires. However, vampires are difficult to kill. The best weapon against a vampire is the sun. In many myths, sunlight burns and kills vampires. In some stories, humans can kill a vampire with a wooden stake. This piece of wood has a pointed end. People drive it through the vampire's heart.

Myths also tell ways to protect against vampires. For example, legend says that vampires are afraid of garlic. Setting out garlic can keep vampires away. Or, people can put seeds by the door of their house. Vampires must stop and count the seeds before they can come in. That gives the people time to escape.

FUN FACT
In some stories, vampire hunters try to find and kill vampires.

WEREWOLF

Beast of the Night

The moon is full. In the forest, a man cries out in pain. He falls to the ground. His arms and legs grow. His ears become pointed. They slide to the top of his head. His nose turns into a snarling snout. Thick fur covers his body.

A werewolf stands where the man had been. The beast lets out a loud howl toward the moon. Then he runs through the trees. Before long, he spots a herd of sheep in a field. The werewolf darts toward them. He catches a lamb in his mouth. He sinks his claws and teeth into the animal. He gobbles it up and runs away.

Like real wolves, werewolves are nocturnal. They typically come out at night.

Werewolves may hunt alone or in packs.

Spreading the Legend

Stories of werewolves have existed for thousands of years. In folklore, a werewolf is a human who turns into a wolf. This behavior is called shape-shifting.

Many shape-shifting myths exist around the world. Werewolf myths are popular in Europe. Europe is home to a large wolf population. Other parts of the world don't have wolves. In these regions' myths, humans turn into other predators. In Africa, people tell stories of were-crocodiles and were-lions. Russia has tales of both werewolves and were-bears.

Stories of werewolves may have started because of disease. A rare disease can cause thick hair to grow on a person's body and face. The disease might have led to werewolf myths.

Or, the myths may have been inspired by rabies. People get this disease from animal bites. People who are sick with rabies may foam at the mouth. They may also become excited or angry. Long ago, people didn't know that germs caused diseases. They might have created werewolf myths to explain these symptoms.

In the past, people often thought

An illustration from 1857 shows a werewolf attacking a human.

A statue of a kitsune guards the famous Ikuta Shrine in Japan.

werewolves were real. They blamed werewolves for missing or dead livestock. Some people even killed humans who were suspected of being werewolves.

Today, few people believe in werewolves. But werewolf stories are still popular. Werewolves appear in many scary books and movies.

FUN FACT
The kitsune appears in Japanese myths. This shape-shifter changes between a human and a fox.

Transformation

According to legend, humans can become werewolves in several ways. Often, the person has no choice. A bite from a werewolf causes the human to transform. The person turns into a werewolf during a full moon.

In other stories, people decide to shape-shift into werewolves. They can transform whenever they want to. But they need

The full moon often triggers a werewolf's wild side.

the right clothing. In German myths, for example, the human must put on a belt made of wolf skin. If the belt falls off, the werewolf turns back into a human. Some werewolves take off their clothes to transform. To return to human form, they put their clothes back on.

The transformation from human to werewolf can be painful. The human's nose turns into a snout. The ears grow pointed. The person's front teeth become sharp. Bones stretch, and fur sprouts all over the body. The person's hands and feet turn into paws. He or she even grows long claws.

A werewolf can take up to three hours to go through a transformation.

Werewolf Traits

In many stories, werewolves look exactly like large wolves. But in some versions, werewolves keep some human traits. For example, they may walk on two legs. Or they may speak with human voices. Some werewolves keep nearly all of their human traits. But they are hairier and stronger than usual.

In addition, some werewolves have wolf traits in their human form. They might have long fingernails and hair. Or their eyebrows might meet in the middle. Long ago, people with these traits were sometimes accused of being werewolves.

In human form, werewolves act normally. But in wolf form, their behavior changes. They often become wild and violent. In many

Some werewolves transform completely into animals. Others look like humans with fur.

Many werewolves have glowing eyes that help them see in the dark.

stories, werewolves are dangerous. They roam around forests and towns. They hunt humans and animals. In fact, many werewolves are evil. As a result, people sometimes fight or kill them.

In some myths, werewolves are easy to kill. In others, humans must shoot them with a silver bullet. If a werewolf is injured, its wound appears in its human form. This makes the werewolf easier to spot.

FUN FACT
In some stories, humans can cure werewolves. Calling a werewolf by its human name can turn it back into a person.

GLOSSARY

anvil
A large block of metal with a flat top that workers use to shape metal.

barnacles
Small sea creatures with shells that attach themselves to surfaces.

chariots
Two-wheeled carts pulled by horses or other animals.

consequences
The results of a choice or an action.

constellation
A group of stars that form a shape.

cultures
Groups of people and the ways they live, including their customs, beliefs, and laws.

duel
To fight or have a contest with someone.

folklore
Traditional beliefs and stories that are passed down by a group of people over time.

folktales
Stories that have been told out loud for many years.

fossils
Remains of plants and animals that lived millions of years ago.

historian
A person who studies and writes about the past.

independence
The ability to make decisions on one's own, without being controlled by others.

Indigenous
Having ancestors who lived in a region before colonists arrived.

Inuit
People who are native to the northern parts of Canada, Alaska, and Greenland.

legends
Well-known stories from the past. Some legends are based on facts, but not all legends are true.

livestock
Animals kept and cared for by humans. Examples include sheep, cows, and chickens.

Middle Ages
A period in European history that lasted from the 400s CE to the 1400s CE.

mischievous

Liking to cause trouble.

mythology

A culture's traditional stories that explain the world in some way.

myths

Well-known stories from the past that often include magic.

Norse

Related to Norway or other parts of Scandinavia.

ointment

A skin cream used for medical purposes.

ore

A material that people use as a source of metal.

possess

To take control of someone's body, often making the body do or say things.

rumors

Stories that are spread by many people but may not actually be true.

samples

Small pieces taken from a larger object or living thing for study.

Scandinavia

An area in northern Europe that includes the countries of Norway, Sweden, and Denmark. Finland and Iceland may also be included.

symbols

Objects or ideas that stand for and remind people of something else.

symptoms

Signs of an illness or disease.

tradition

A way of doing something that is passed down over many years.

UFO

Short for "unidentified flying object." A mysterious thing people see in the sky and sometimes believe is a spaceship.

underworld

The land of the dead.

Western

Coming from or shaped by the people and ideas of Europe and North America.

TO LEARN MORE

Books

Halls, Kelly Milner. *Cryptid Creatures: A Field Guide*. Sasquatch Books, 2019.

Krensky, Stephen. *The Book of Mythical Beasts & Magical Creatures*. DK Publishing, 2020.

Lawrence, Sandra. *The Atlas of Monsters: Mythical Creatures from Around the World*. Running Press Kids, 2019.

Menzies, Jean. *Greek Myths: Meet the Heroes, Gods, and Monsters of Ancient Greece*. DK Publishing, 2020.

Napoli, Donna Jo. *Treasury of Magical Tales from Around the World*. National Geographic Kids, 2021.

Nordvig, Mathias. *Norse Mythology for Kids: Tales of Gods, Creatures, and Quests*. Rockridge Press, 2020.

Online Resources

American Museum of Natural History: "Mythic Creatures"
https://www.amnh.org/exhibitions/mythic-creatures

Kids Britannica: "Animals, Legendary"
https://kids.britannica.com/kids/article/animals-legendary/352758

National Geographic Kids: "Five Terrifying Tales from Greek Mythology"
https://www.natgeokids.com/uk/discover/history/greece/greek-myths/

Wonderopolis: "Is There Any Proof That Bigfoot Is Real?"
https://wonderopolis.org/wonder/is-there-any-proof-that-bigfoot-is-real

INDEX

PHOTO CREDITS